SRI LANKA

BUDGET TRAVEL GUIDE

2023

Discover the Magic on a Shoestring: Unleash Your Wanderlust as a First-Time Budget Traveler in Sri Lanka!

WARDENS FEET

COPYRIGHT©2023 WARDENS FEET

ALL RIGHTS RESERVED

TABLE OF CONTENTS

INTRODUCTION TO SRI LANKA 6

CHAPTER 1 10
- GEOGRAPHY AND CLIMATE 10
- CULTURAL DIVERSITY AND TRADITIONS 12
- TOP ATTRACTIONS AND MUST-VISIT PLACES 15

CHAPTER 2 18
- PLANNING YOUR TRIP 18
  - *Setting a Budget* 18
  - *Choosing the Right Time to Visit* 19
  - *Obtaining Necessary Travel Documents and Visa Information* 21
  - *Vaccinations and Health Precautions* 24

CHAPTER 3 26
- TRANSPORTATION IN SRI LANKA 26
  - *Getting to Sri Lanka* 26
  - *Domestic Transportation Options (Buses, Trains, Tuk-tuks, etc.)* 28
  - *Tips for Navigating Transportation on a Budget* 30

CHAPTER 4 34
- ACCOMMODATION OPTIONS 34
  - *Budget-Friendly Accommodations (Hostels, Guesthouses, Home-stays)* 34
  - *Tips for Booking Affordable Places to Stay* 36

CHAPTER 5 38
- FOOD AND DINING 38
  - *Local Cuisine and Must-Try Dishes* 38
  - *Budget-Friendly Eating Options (Street Food, Local Markets, "Rice and Curry" meals)* 39
  - *Drinking Water and Food Safety Tips* 41

CHAPTER 6 44

- Budget-Friendly Activities and Sightseeing 44
  - Free and Low-Cost Attractions 44
  - Hiking and Nature Exploration on a Budget 46
  - Cultural Shows and Festivals 48

CHAPTER 7 52

- Money-Saving Tips and Tricks 52
  - Bargaining and Negotiating Prices 52
  - Using Public Facilities Wisely 53
  - Understanding Local Customs to Avoid Extra Expenses 55

CHAPTER 8 58

- Safety and Travel Precautions 58
  - General Safety Tips for Tourists 58
  - Health and Hygiene Precautions 59
  - Avoiding Scams and Tourist Traps 61

CHAPTER 9 64

- Sustainable Tourism in Sri Lanka 64
  - Responsible Travel Practices 64
  - Supporting Local Communities and Conservation Efforts 66

CHAPTER 10 70

- Basic Local Phrases and Cultural Etiquette 70
  - Useful Phrases in Sinhala and Tamil 70
  - Cultural Dos and Don'ts for Respectful Travel 72

CHAPTER 11 76

- Packing Essentials for a Budget Trip 76
  - Clothing and Weather Considerations 76
  - Essential Items and Gadgets 79
  - Packing Light and Smart 82

CONCLUSION AND FINAL TIPS 86

- Recap of Key Points 86
- Embracing the Adventure: Final Thoughts on Budget Travel in Sri Lanka 88

INTRODUCTION TO SRI LANKA

As I stepped onto the emerald jewel of the Indian Ocean, I was instantly bewitched by the enchanting charm of Sri Lanka. Picture-perfect landscapes unfurled before me, each scene painted with vibrant hues that seemed to dance in harmony with the rhythm of the island. It was a symphony of colors and flavors, and I was eager to immerse myself in this kaleidoscope of experiences.

My journey began in Colombo, the bustling capital city that embraced both modernity and tradition. Tuk-tuks zipped through the streets like nimble fireflies, navigating the chaotic yet captivating traffic. The aromas of spicy street food wafted through the air, beckoning me to try every savory bite. With a sense of adventure, I tasted mouthwatering kottu roti, sizzling deviled prawns, and the fiery heat of a traditional hoppers breakfast. The culinary extravaganza alone was enough to ignite my taste buds and keep me yearning for more.

Leaving the urban charm behind, I ventured to the serene countryside, where lush tea plantations carpeted the rolling hills like a vast, green ocean. It was as if the landscape had been carefully quilted, with rows of tea bushes stretching out like verdant waves. The iconic Ceylon tea was born here, and I couldn't resist taking a tour of one of the tea factories, learning about the time-honored process that yields that distinctive aroma and flavor. Sipping a steaming cup of freshly brewed tea while gazing out at the endless sea of green was an experience that warmed both my heart and soul.

As I explored further, I found myself in the sacred city of Kandy, a treasure trove of spiritual wonders. The Temple of the Tooth, a sacred relic of Lord Buddha's tooth, stood majestically, exuding an aura of mystery and reverence. The rhythmic beating of traditional drums during an enchanting Kandyan dance performance seemed to echo the very pulse of the island. I felt like an integral part of a timeless tale, where the present merged seamlessly with a storied past.

The journey took me to Sigiriya, where a colossal rock fortress rose defiantly, its presence looming large against the horizon. Climbing to the top, I marveled at the breathtaking views, feeling as if I had ascended to the heavens. The ancient frescoes adorned the rock walls, depicting captivating stories that whispered secrets of the past. It was as though I had entered an ancient kingdom, where the legends of kings and queens unfolded before my very eyes.

With an adrenaline rush craving, I set forth to the coastal paradise of Mirissa, where the azure waters embraced the golden shores. The gentle waves lured me into their embrace, and I found myself enveloped in the salty splendor of the Indian Ocean. Swimming alongside majestic sea turtles and witnessing playful dolphins dance on the water's surface filled my heart with an indescribable joy. The setting sun painted the sky in shades of pink and orange, casting a mesmerizing spell that left me in awe of nature's artistry.

Throughout my journey, I encountered the warm-hearted locals who welcomed me with open arms. Their genuine smiles and hospitable nature made me feel like an old friend returning home. Engaging in conversations with them, I gained insights into their way of life, their deep-rooted traditions, and their hopes and dreams for the future.

Sri Lanka, the pearl of the Indian Ocean, has imprinted itself on my soul forever. Its tapestry of experiences, from the buzzing streets of Colombo to the tranquil tea estates, from the ancient marvels to the coastal delights, has left an indelible mark on my heart. The island's kaleidoscope of colors, flavors, and emotions has woven a narrative that continues to resonate with me. To any first-time budget traveler seeking a destination that combines adventure, culture, and soul-stirring moments, I say, set your compass towards Sri Lanka, and prepare to be captivated by the magic it holds. Embrace the journey, and let the island work its enchantment on you.

CHAPTER 1

Geography and Climate

Nestled in the heart of the Indian Ocean, Sri Lanka is a paradise for nature lovers and adventure seekers alike. Its unique geography offers a diverse landscape that ranges from pristine beaches to misty mountains and lush rainforests. The island is a tropical haven, brimming with awe-inspiring vistas that will leave any traveler in absolute awe.

As I journeyed through this land of wonder, I found myself enchanted by the sheer variety of natural beauty that unfolded before my eyes. The coastal regions, adorned with golden sands and swaying palm trees, beckoned me to soak in the warm embrace of the sun. The turquoise waters gently lapping at the shore invited me for a refreshing dip, making every beach visit a rejuvenating experience.

Venturing inland, I was captivated by the majestic hill country. The rolling hills, dressed in velvety carpets of tea plantations, painted a tranquil and soothing landscape. As I ascended higher, the air became cooler, and the mist embraced the surroundings like a mystical shroud. The mountains hid within their embrace charming little towns like Ella and Nuwara Eliya, each offering breathtaking panoramic views that made me feel like I was on top of the world.

Sri Lanka's geography also gifted the island with lush rainforests, such as the famous Sinharaja Forest Reserve. The vibrant flora and fauna that thrived within its depths painted an exquisite tapestry of green. I trekked through the forest, accompanied by the melodious symphony of birds and the whispering of leaves, feeling like I had stepped into a real-life Eden.

With such diversity in landscape, the climate of Sri Lanka also varies from region to region. Along the coasts, I basked in the warmth of a tropical climate, where the sun embraced me like an old friend. The coastal areas are perfect for those seeking endless summer days, perfect for sunbathing, surfing, and beach strolls.

As I ventured into the central regions, the hill country introduced me to a cooler and more temperate climate, offering a pleasant escape from the heat of the coast. Misty mornings and gentle drizzles became the norm, transforming the hills into an ethereal wonderland.

One of the most fascinating aspects of Sri Lanka's climate is the presence of two monsoon seasons, which affect different parts of the island at different times of the year. The southwest monsoon brings rain to the southwestern coast and hill country from May to September, while the northeast monsoon blesses the northern and eastern regions with rainfall from November to February. Planning my travels around these monsoon patterns allowed me to make the most of my journey and explore the diverse regions without being caught in the rain.

Cultural Diversity and Traditions

As I delved deeper into the heart of Sri Lanka, I discovered a rich tapestry of cultural diversity and traditions that has been woven over millennia. The island's history is a captivating narrative of conquests, trade, and migration, resulting in a vibrant melting pot of cultures that make it a treasure trove for any curious traveler.

Sri Lanka's people are as diverse as its landscapes. The Sinhalese, who form the majority, have a warm and welcoming nature that makes you feel like a cherished guest in their homeland. Their language, Sinhala, is a beautiful melody that dances on the tongue, and I couldn't resist picking up a few phrases to connect more deeply with the locals during my travels.

The Tamil community, concentrated predominantly in the northern and eastern regions of the island, brings its own distinct traditions and customs. Their graceful demeanor and devotion to their unique cultural practices added yet another layer of fascination to my Sri Lankan journey.

Beyond the Sinhalese and Tamil communities, Sri Lanka embraces a kaleidoscope of ethnicities, including the Moor, Burgher, and Malay communities. Each group has preserved its heritage with pride, contributing its flavors to the rich cultural fabric of the island.

One of the most captivating aspects of Sri Lanka's cultural diversity is its religious heritage. Buddhism, with its ancient roots, holds a special place in the hearts of the people. Temples, stupas, and statues of Lord Buddha stand proudly across the island, exuding an air of serenity and wisdom. Visiting the sacred Temple of the Tooth in Kandy was a profound experience, where I felt humbled by the devotion and spirituality that seemed to permeate the very air.

Apart from Buddhism, Sri Lanka is also home to significant Hindu, Muslim, and Christian communities. The magnificent Hindu temples, adorned with intricate carvings and vibrant colors, transported me to a realm of mystical devotion. The colorful festivals and processions held in honor of Hindu deities left me mesmerized, where tradition and faith merged in a joyous celebration of life.

The friendly and hospitable nature of the Sri Lankan people became most apparent during my stay in a rural village. I was fortunate to witness traditional ceremonies and rituals that offered a glimpse into the heart of their culture. The villagers' generous spirit was evident in the warmth of their smiles and the inviting aroma of home-cooked meals they shared with me.

The arts and craftsmanship of Sri Lanka are also steeped in its cultural heritage. From intricate handwoven textiles to exquisite woodcarvings and brassware, each creation tells a story of skilled craftsmanship passed down through generations. Visiting local artisan workshops not only allowed me to witness their talent firsthand but also gave me the opportunity to support their livelihoods and preserve these age-old traditions.

Sri Lanka's festivals are a testament to the island's vibrant cultural scene. The exuberant Kandy Esala Perahera, a grand procession that takes place in Kandy, captivated me with its dazzling display of traditional dance, music, and ornately decorated elephants. I felt as if I had been transported back in time to a bygone era of royal splendor and pageantry.

Throughout my journey, I learned that Sri Lanka's cultural diversity and traditions form an intricate mosaic, with each piece contributing its unique beauty to the whole. The island's ability to harmoniously blend ancient customs with modern influences is a testament to the resilience of its people and the richness of its heritage.

Top Attractions and Must-Visit Places

Prepare to be mesmerized by the myriad of top attractions and must-visit places that Sri Lanka has to offer. This island gem is a treasure trove of diverse landscapes, ancient wonders, and natural beauty, promising an unforgettable adventure that will leave you in awe of its splendor.

Sigiriya Rock Fortress: A UNESCO World Heritage Site, Sigiriya is an ancient rock fortress that rises majestically from the plains. Climb to the top through the mesmerizing Lion's Paw entrance and be rewarded with breathtaking views of the surrounding countryside and the remnants of a once-glorious palace.

Dambulla Cave Temple: Explore the ancient cave temples of Dambulla, adorned with stunning Buddha statues and intricate frescoes that depict the life of Lord Buddha. This sacred site holds a spiritual allure that resonates with visitors of all beliefs.

Temple of the Tooth, Kandy: Immerse yourself in the spiritual heart of Sri Lanka by visiting the Temple of the Tooth in Kandy. This sacred temple houses a relic of Lord Buddha's tooth, making it a significant pilgrimage site and the center of grand festivals.

Galle Fort: Step back in time and stroll through the cobblestone streets of Galle Fort, a UNESCO-listed heritage site. The well-preserved fortifications, charming colonial architecture, and vibrant atmosphere make this a delightful destination.

Yala National Park: Embark on an exhilarating safari adventure in Yala National Park, home to a variety of wildlife, including elephants, leopards, and a plethora of bird species. The thrill of encountering these majestic creatures in their natural habitat is truly unforgettable.

Ella: Nestled amidst the misty hill country, the quaint town of Ella offers breathtaking views of the lush tea plantations and cascading waterfalls. Hike up to Ella Rock or Little Adam's Peak to witness some of the most stunning vistas in Sri Lanka.

Adam's Peak (Sri Pada): Embark on a spiritual and physical journey by climbing Adam's Peak, a sacred mountain revered by multiple faiths. The awe-inspiring sunrise view from the summit is a reward that words can hardly do justice.

Mirissa: Unwind in the coastal haven of Mirissa, where golden beaches and azure waters invite you to relax and rejuvenate. Don't miss the opportunity to witness magnificent blue whales and playful dolphins on a thrilling whale-watching excursion.

Nuwara Eliya: Experience the charm of "Little England" in Nuwara Eliya, a hill station with a distinct colonial ambiance. Enjoy a leisurely boat ride on Lake Gregory or savor the flavors of Ceylon tea at a nearby plantation.

Polonnaruwa: Unearth the ancient glory of Polonnaruwa, a UNESCO World Heritage Site boasting well-preserved ruins of an ancient royal capital. Explore the vast archaeological park, which houses remarkable structures like Gal Vihara and the Royal Palace complex.

Bentota: Indulge in serenity and luxury in Bentota, a coastal paradise with palm-fringed beaches and a wide range of water sports activities. Treat yourself to a relaxing spa session or a soothing boat ride on the Bentota River.

Horton Plains National Park: Lace up your hiking boots and explore the ethereal beauty of Horton Plains National Park. The enchanting Worlds End viewpoint offers a jaw-dropping panorama of the seemingly endless plains and deep valleys.

CHAPTER 2

Planning Your Trip

Setting a Budget

Accommodation: You can find budget-friendly accommodation in Sri Lanka, such as hostels, guesthouses, and homestays. A dorm bed in a hostel will typically cost around $10-15 per night, while a private room in a guesthouse will cost around $20-30 per night.

Food: Sri Lankan food is delicious and affordable. You can get a filling meal for around $5-10. If you want to save money, you can cook your own meals or eat street food.

Transportation: Public transportation in Sri Lanka is cheap and efficient. You can get around by bus, train, or tuk-tuk. A bus ticket will typically cost around $1-2, while a train ticket will cost around $2-5. A tuk-tuk ride will cost around $2-5 for a short distance.

Activities: There are many free or low-cost activities to do in Sri Lanka, such as visiting temples, exploring the beaches, and hiking in the mountains. If you want to do some paid activities, such as visiting national parks or going on a safari, you can expect to pay around $20-50 per person.

Here is a sample budget for a 7-day trip to Sri Lanka on a budget:

Accommodation: $100

Food: $100

Transportation: $50

Activities: $50

Other expenses: $50

Total: $350

This budget is just a starting point, and you may be able to save money or spend more depending on your travel style. For example, if you want to stay in nicer accommodations or do more expensive activities, you will need to increase your budget. However, if you are willing to stay in budget accommodations, cook your own meals, and take public transportation, you can easily travel to Sri Lanka on a budget of $350 per person per week.

Choosing the Right Time to Visit

When it comes to choosing the right time to visit Sri Lanka, the island's climate and weather patterns play a crucial role in shaping your travel experience. Each season brings its own unique charm, allowing you to tailor your trip to match your preferences and desired activities.

Peak Season (December to March): Sri Lanka's peak season, falling between December and March, is the most popular time for tourists. The weather during this period is generally dry and pleasant, making it ideal for beach vacations and exploring the cultural attractions. The west and south coasts, including places like Colombo, Galle, and Mirissa, are perfect for soaking up the sun and indulging in water sports. Additionally, the hill country, such as Nuwara Eliya and Ella, offers a refreshing escape from the heat, with cool temperatures and lush landscapes. However, be prepared for larger crowds and higher accommodation prices during this peak season.

Shoulder Season (April and September to November): The shoulder seasons of April and September to November are also excellent times to visit Sri Lanka. The weather remains relatively dry and pleasant, offering a mix of sunny days and occasional rain showers. During these months, you can still enjoy the beaches and outdoor activities, but with fewer crowds and more budget-friendly options for accommodation and tours. April is especially ideal for witnessing the Sinhala and Tamil New Year celebrations, which provide a fascinating glimpse into Sri Lanka's rich cultural traditions.

Monsoon Season (May to August in the Southwest, October to January in the Northeast): Sri Lanka experiences two monsoon seasons, which affect different regions of the island at different times of the year. The southwest monsoon brings rain to the southwestern coast and hill country from May to August, while the northeast monsoon affects the northern and eastern regions from October to January. During these months, certain areas may experience heavy rainfall and potential disruptions to outdoor activities. However, the monsoon season also brings a lush and vibrant landscape, making it an excellent time to explore the rainforests and waterfalls in their full glory.

Ultimately, the right time to visit Sri Lanka depends on your preferences, interests, and tolerance for weather conditions. If you prefer sunny and dry weather with bustling tourist activity, the peak season is perfect for you. On the other hand, if you seek a more tranquil experience with potential savings on accommodations, the shoulder seasons offer a great compromise. And for those who appreciate the allure of lush landscapes and don't mind occasional rain, the monsoon season presents a unique opportunity to explore Sri Lanka in a different light.

Obtaining Necessary Travel Documents and Visa Information

Passport: Your passport must be valid for at least 6 months beyond your intended stay in Sri Lanka.

Visa: Most nationalities, including citizens of the United States, Canada, the United Kingdom, and the European Union, can obtain a visa on arrival in Sri Lanka. The visa fee is $35 USD.

Proof of Financial Means: You will need to show proof that you have enough money to support yourself during your stay in Sri Lanka. This can be a letter from your bank showing that you have a balance of at least $500 USD, or a credit card statement showing that you have a credit limit of at least $1000 USD.

Proof of onward travel: You will need to show proof that you have a valid onward ticket out of Sri Lanka. This can be a copy of your flight ticket, or a letter from your travel agent confirming your onward travel arrangements.

Other documents: You may also be asked to provide other documents, such as a copy of your itinerary, a letter of invitation from a friend or relative in Sri Lanka, or a proof of accommodation.

You can apply for a visa on arrival at any of the following Sri Lankan airports:

Bandaranaike International Airport (Colombo)

Mattala Rajapaksa International Airport (Hambantota)

Jaffna International Airport (Jaffna)

Trincomalee International Airport (Trincomalee)

The visa on arrival process is usually quick and easy, but it is a good idea to have all of your documents ready in advance.

Here are some additional tips for obtaining travel documents and visas for Sri Lanka:

Start the process early: It is a good idea to start the process of obtaining your travel documents and visas at least 6 weeks before your intended travel date. This will give you plenty of time to gather all of the necessary documents and to apply for your visa, if necessary.

Check the requirements: The visa requirements for Sri Lanka can change from time to time, so it is important to check the latest requirements before you travel. You can find the latest visa requirements on the website of the Sri Lankan Department of Immigration and Emigration.

Apply online: If you are eligible, you can apply for a visa online through the Sri Lankan Department of Immigration and Emigration website. This is a convenient way to apply for your visa, and it can help you to avoid the long queues at the airport.

Vaccinations and Health Precautions

Hepatitis A: Hepatitis A is a viral infection that can cause liver inflammation. It is a common illness in developing countries, and it can be spread through contaminated food and water. You can get vaccinated against hepatitis A.

Hepatitis B: Hepatitis B is another viral infection that can cause liver inflammation. It is a serious illness, and it can be spread through blood and body fluids. You can get vaccinated against hepatitis B.

Rabies: Rabies is a viral infection that can be fatal if it is not treated. It is transmitted via the bite of an animal that is diseased. You can get vaccinated against rabies.

Typhoid: Typhoid is a bacterial infection that can cause fever, headache, and diarrhea. It spreads by tainted water and food. You can get vaccinated against typhoid.

Diphtheria, Tetanus, and Pertussis (DTP): DTP is a vaccine that protects against three diseases: diphtheria, tetanus, and pertussis. These diseases are all serious, and they can be fatal. You should get a DTP booster every 10 years.

Measles, Mumps, and Rubella (MMR): MMR is a vaccine that protects against three diseases: measles, mumps, and rubella. These diseases are all contagious, and they can be serious. You should get a MMR booster every 20 years.

Polio: Paralysis may result from the viral illness polio. It is a serious illness, and it can be fatal. Polio has been eradicated in most countries, but it is still a problem in some parts of the world. You should get a polio booster every 10 years.

Insect repellent: Insect repellent is important for preventing mosquito bites. Mosquitoes can carry illnesses like the Zika virus, dengue fever, and malaria. Use insect repellent with picaridin or DEET in it.

Malaria medication: If you are traveling to areas where malaria is present, you should take malaria medication. Malaria is a serious illness, and it can be fatal. There are different types of malaria medication, so talk to your doctor about which one is right for you.

Water purification: If you are not sure if the water is safe to drink, you should purify it. You can use a water filter or a water purification tablet.

Sunscreen: Sunscreen is crucial for shielding your skin from the sun's damaging rays. The sun's rays can cause skin cancer, so it is important to wear sunscreen every day, even if it is cloudy.

CHAPTER 3

Transportation in Sri Lanka

Getting to Sri Lanka

Getting to the enchanting island of Sri Lanka is a seamless process, thanks to its well-connected international airports and strategic location in the Indian Ocean. Whether you're arriving from neighboring countries or distant continents, there are several convenient options to choose from.

By Air: Bandaranaike International Airport (BIA) in Colombo is Sri Lanka's main international gateway. Situated about 35 kilometers north of Colombo, BIA receives flights from major cities across Asia, Europe, the Middle East, and Australia. It is well-served by numerous international airlines, making it easy to find direct flights or convenient connections from various destinations around the world. Additionally, there are smaller international airports in cities like Mattala and Jaffna, which cater to limited international flights.

By Sea: While air travel is the most common way to reach Sri Lanka, there are also options for arriving by sea. The Colombo Port is a major hub for cruise ships and cargo vessels. Some luxury cruise lines offer itineraries that include Colombo as a port of call, allowing travelers to embark on a unique journey that combines sea travel with exploring the island's wonders.

Visa Requirements: Before planning your trip, ensure you have the necessary travel documents, including a valid passport and a visa to enter Sri Lanka. Depending on your nationality, you may be eligible for a visa on arrival or an electronic visa (ETA) that can be obtained online in advance. Make sure to check the latest visa regulations and requirements for your country before booking your flight.

Domestic Transportation: Once you've landed in Colombo, Sri Lanka's domestic transportation options make it easy to explore various regions of the island. Buses, trains, and domestic flights connect major cities and tourist destinations, offering affordable and convenient ways to travel within the country. Buses are the most common mode of transportation for locals and budget travelers, while trains offer scenic journeys through the hill country and coastal regions. For quicker connections between distant destinations, domestic flights are available from Colombo to various cities.

Transportation from the Airport: From Bandaranaike International Airport, you can easily reach Colombo city center and other destinations via taxis, airport shuttles, or ride-hailing services. The airport has well-organized transportation facilities to ensure a smooth transition to your desired location.

Travel Tips:

It's advisable to book your flights well in advance, especially during the peak tourist season, to secure the best fares and options.

Keep important travel documents and valuables in a secure place while traveling to and from the airport.

Familiarize yourself with Sri Lanka's customs regulations to avoid any issues during entry or exit.

Stay updated on any travel advisories or health-related requirements issued by your home country or Sri Lanka's authorities before and during your journey.

Domestic Transportation Options (Buses, Trains, Tuk-tuks, etc.)

Buses: Buses are the most common form of transportation in Sri Lanka. They are cheap and efficient, and they can take you to most places in the country. There are two main types of buses in Sri Lanka: public buses and private buses. Public buses are run by the Sri Lanka Transport Board (SLTB), and they are the cheapest option. Private buses are run by private companies, and they are slightly more expensive than public buses.

Trains: Trains are another popular option for transportation in Sri Lanka. They are not as cheap as buses, but they are more comfortable and scenic. The Sri Lanka Railways operates a network of trains that covers most of the country.

Tuk-tuks: Tuk-tuks are small, three-wheeled vehicles that are a popular way to get around in Sri Lanka. They are very cheap, but they can be a bit crowded and noisy. Tuk-tuks are not metered, so it is important to agree on a price before you get in.

Taxis: Taxis are a more expensive option, but they are more comfortable than tuk-tuks. Taxis are metered, so you will know how much you are paying before you get in.

Ride-hailing apps: There are a number of ride-hailing apps available in Sri Lanka, such as Uber and PickMe. These apps are a convenient way to get around, and they are often cheaper than taxis.

If you are on a budget, buses and trains are the best way to get around Sri Lanka. They are cheap and efficient, and they can take you to most places in the country. Tuk-tuks and taxis are more expensive, but they are more comfortable and convenient. Ride-hailing apps are a good option if you are traveling in a group or if you need to get to a specific location quickly.

Here are some tips for using domestic transportation in Sri Lanka:

Do your research: Before you travel, it is a good idea to do some research on the different transportation options available. This will enable you to select the best solution for you.

Be prepared to bargain: If you are taking a tuk-tuk or taxi, be prepared to bargain with the driver over the price. This is common practice in Sri Lanka, and it is a good way to get a good deal.

Be aware of your surroundings: When you are traveling in a bus or train, be aware of your surroundings. Keep your possessions close to hand and watch out for pickpockets.

Have fun! Traveling around Sri Lanka is a great way to experience the country. Soak up the atmosphere, meet new people, and enjoy the journey.

Tips for Navigating Transportation on a Budget

Use public transportation: Buses and trains are the cheapest way to get around Sri Lanka. They are efficient and can take you to most places in the country.

Bargain with tuk-tuk drivers: Tuk-tuks are a popular way to get around in Sri Lanka, but they can be expensive. Be prepared to bargain with the driver over the price before you get in.

Use ride-hailing apps: There are a number of ride-hailing apps available in Sri Lanka, such as Uber and PickMe. These apps are a convenient way to get around, and they are often cheaper than taxis.

Consider staying in a hostel: Hostels are an excellent way to save money on lodging. They offer shared rooms and bathrooms, and they are a great way to meet other travelers.

Cook your own meals: Eating out can be expensive in Sri Lanka. Prep your own meals if you want to save money. There are many affordable grocery stores in Sri Lanka, and you can find fresh produce and spices at local markets.

Visit free attractions: There are many free attractions in Sri Lanka, such as temples, beaches, and national parks. These are a great way to see the country and save money on your trip.

Start your research early: Before you travel, it is a good idea to do some research on the different transportation options available. This will enable you to select the best solution for you.

Be flexible with your plans: Things don't always go according to plan when you're traveling, so it's important to be flexible with your plans. If one transportation option doesn't work out, be prepared to try another one.

Get assistance: Do not be afraid to seek for assistance if you are lost or confused. Locals are usually very friendly and helpful, and they will be happy to point you in the right direction.

CHAPTER 4

Accommodation Options

Budget-Friendly Accommodations (Hostels, Guesthouses, Home-stays)

In Sri Lanka, budget-friendly accommodations are plentiful, catering to the needs of thrifty travelers without compromising on comfort and hospitality. Whether you prefer the communal atmosphere of hostels, the local charm of guesthouses, or the intimate experience of home-stays, there are plenty of affordable options to choose from.

Hostels: Hostels are an excellent choice for budget travelers seeking a social and vibrant atmosphere. They are abundant in popular tourist destinations, especially in Colombo, Kandy, Ella, and Mirissa. Dormitory-style rooms offer the most economical rates, allowing you to meet fellow travelers and share experiences. Many hostels also provide private rooms at a slightly higher cost for those seeking more privacy. Additionally, hostels often organize communal activities, making it easy to connect with like-minded individuals and explore the local culture together.

Guesthouses: Guesthouses are another budget-friendly accommodation option found throughout Sri Lanka. They are usually family-run establishments, providing a warm and personalized experience. Guesthouses range from simple to more comfortable settings, and the prices are generally lower than hotels. In addition to private rooms, some guesthouses offer shared facilities, making them a cost-effective choice for solo travelers or small groups. You'll often find guesthouses in both urban and rural areas, offering a chance to experience authentic Sri Lankan hospitality.

Home-stays: Home-stays provide a unique opportunity to immerse yourself in the local way of life and culture. These accommodations allow you to stay with a Sri Lankan family in their home, offering a more intimate and personal experience. Home-stays are particularly common in rural areas, where you can escape the hustle and bustle of city life and discover the island's tranquil charm. You'll get a taste of traditional Sri Lankan cuisine and customs while forming lasting connections with your hosts.

Eco-Lodges and Guesthouses: For eco-conscious travelers, Sri Lanka has a growing number of eco-lodges and eco-friendly guesthouses. These accommodations focus on sustainability and minimizing their impact on the environment. Staying in an eco-lodge not only supports responsible tourism but also provides a unique experience surrounded by nature and wildlife.

Online Booking Platforms: To find the best budget-friendly accommodations, utilize online booking platforms and read reviews from previous guests. Websites like Booking.com, Hostelworld, and Airbnb offer a wide range of options, allowing you to compare prices and amenities to suit your preferences and budget.

Negotiation and Walk-Ins: In Sri Lanka, it's often possible to negotiate room rates, especially during the low season or when booking for an extended stay. If you're comfortable with spontaneity, consider walking into guesthouses or home-stays without prior reservations, as they might offer discounted rates for last-minute bookings.

Tips for Booking Affordable Places to Stay

Consider staying in hostels: Hostels are a great way to save money on accommodation. They offer shared rooms and bathrooms, and they are a great way to meet other travelers.

Look for homestays: Homestays are a great way to experience local culture and save money on accommodation. You will stay with a local family and share their home, meals, and experiences.

Book in advance: If you are traveling during peak season, it is important to book your accommodation in advance. This will help you to get the best deals and avoid disappointment.

Use online booking sites: There are a number of online booking sites that can help you to find affordable accommodation in Sri Lanka. These sites often have discounts and deals, so it is worth checking them out.

Negotiate the price: If you are staying in a guesthouse or hotel, be prepared to negotiate the price. This is common practice in Sri Lanka, and it is a good way to get a good deal.

Stay in less popular areas: If you are on a tight budget, you may want to consider staying in less popular areas. These areas are often just as beautiful as the more popular tourist destinations, but they are less crowded and cheaper.

Read reviews: Before you book, be sure to read reviews of the accommodation you are considering. You'll have a better understanding of what to anticipate if you do this.

Ask for recommendations: If you know someone who has been to Sri Lanka, ask them for recommendations for affordable places to stay.

Be flexible with your dates: If you are flexible with your dates, you may be able to find better deals on accommodation.

Consider staying in a dorm: If you are traveling solo, consider staying in a dorm. This is a great way to save money on accommodation and meet other travelers.

Chapter 5

Food and Dining

Local Cuisine and Must-Try Dishes

Appam: A type of pancake made with rice flour and coconut milk. It frequently comes with a stew or curry.

Kottu: A stir-fry made with chopped roti bread, vegetables, and meat or seafood. It is a well-liked Sri Lankan street meal.

Dosa: A kind of crepe cooked with a batter of fermented rice and lentils. Chutneys and sambar are frequently served with it.

Sambal: A spicy condiment made with chili peppers, onions, and tomatoes. The usual accompaniments are rice and curry.

Curry: A term used to refer to a variety of dishes in Sri Lanka. Curry dishes typically consist of meat or seafood cooked in a sauce made with spices, coconut milk, and vegetables.

Kiribath: A dish made with milk rice. It is often served on special occasions.

Pol Sambol: A spicy condiment made with coconut, onions, and chili peppers. The usual accompaniments are rice and curry.

Lunu Miris: A spicy chutney made with onions, chili peppers, and lime juice. The usual accompaniments are rice and curry.

These are just a few of the many delicious dishes that you can try in Sri Lanka. Be sure to explore and try new things, as you are sure to find something you love.

Here are some tips for finding local cuisine on a budget in Sri Lanka:

Look for local restaurants: Local restaurants are often the best places to find authentic Sri Lankan cuisine. They are also usually more affordable than tourist restaurants.

Ask for recommendations: If you know someone who has been to Sri Lanka, ask them for recommendations for local restaurants.

Be bold: Do not be hesitant to explore new things. Sri Lankan cuisine is full of delicious and unique dishes, so you're sure to find something you love.

Budget-Friendly Eating Options (Street Food, Local Markets, "Rice and Curry" meals)

Street food: Sri Lanka has a wide variety of delicious street food, and it is a great way to eat on a budget. You can find everything from kottu (a stir-fry made with chopped roti bread, vegetables, and meat or seafood) to hoppers (a type of pancake made with rice flour and coconut milk) to pani puri (a crispy hollow ball filled with mashed potatoes, chickpeas, chutneys, and spices).

Local markets: Local markets are a great place to find fresh produce, spices, and other ingredients for cooking your own meals. You can also find cooked food stalls at many markets, which is a great way to get a delicious and affordable meal.

"Rice and curry" meals: Rice and curry is a staple dish in Sri Lanka, and it is a great way to eat on a budget. You can find rice and curry meals at most restaurants, and they usually include a variety of curries, vegetables, and rice.

Avoid tourist restaurants: Tourist restaurants are often more expensive than local restaurants.

Look for lunch specials: Many restaurants offer lunch specials that are a great way to get a delicious and affordable meal.

Share dishes: Sri Lankan food is often served in large portions, so you can share dishes with your traveling companions to save money.

Cook your own meals: If you are on a tight budget, you can save money by cooking your own meals. There are many affordable grocery stores in Sri Lanka, and you can find fresh produce and spices at local markets.

Drinking Water and Food Safety Tips

Drink bottled water: Tap water in Sri Lanka is not safe to drink, so it is important to drink bottled water. Bottled water is readily available in Sri Lanka, and it is relatively inexpensive.

Avoid ice cubes: Ice cubes in Sri Lanka are often made with tap water, so it is best to avoid them. If you are served ice cubes, ask the waiter if they are made with bottled water.

Be careful with street food: Street food in Sri Lanka is delicious, but it is important to be careful. Some street food vendors may not use safe practices, so it is best to avoid food that has been sitting out in the open or that is not cooked thoroughly.

Cook your own meals: If you are on a tight budget, you can save money by cooking your own meals. There are many affordable grocery stores in Sri Lanka, and you can find fresh produce and spices at local markets.

Wash your hands often: It is important to wash your hands often to prevent the spread of germs. Specifically before eating and right after using the restroom, wash your hands for at least 20 seconds with soap and water.

Ask questions: If you are unsure about whether or not something is safe to eat or drink, ask the waiter or vendor.

They should be able to tell you if the food is made with safe water and if it is cooked properly.

Be aware of your surroundings: When you are eating or drinking in Sri Lanka, be aware of your surroundings. If you see anything that makes you feel uncomfortable, don't be afraid to ask for a different meal or to leave.

Trust your gut: If you are not sure about something, it is always best to err on the side of caution. Don't eat anything that doesn't seem or smell correct.

CHAPTER 6

Budget-Friendly Activities and Sightseeing

Free and Low-Cost Attractions

Sri Lanka is a paradise for budget travelers, offering an array of free and low-cost attractions that allow you to immerse yourself in the island's beauty and culture without breaking the bank. From pristine beaches to ancient ruins, here are some of the top free and affordable experiences to enjoy during your Sri Lankan adventure:

Beach Bliss: Sri Lanka boasts some of the most stunning beaches in the world, and many of them are free to visit. Spend a day basking in the sun and splashing in the turquoise waters of beaches like Mirissa, Unawatuna, and Tangalle. Whether you're a sun-seeker, surfer, or simply a beachcomber, the coastline of Sri Lanka offers something for everyone.

Exploring Ancient Cities: Discover the rich historical legacy of Sri Lanka by exploring ancient cities like Anuradhapura and Polonnaruwa. These UNESCO World Heritage Sites boast well-preserved ruins, ancient stupas, and intricate stone carvings. Entry fees are affordable, and the experience of stepping back in time is invaluable.

Sacred Sites: Visit temples and sacred sites scattered across the island, offering a glimpse into Sri Lanka's deep-rooted spirituality. The Temple of the Tooth in Kandy, Kelaniya Raja Maha Vihara in Colombo, and the Dambulla Cave Temple are just a few examples of the many revered places that welcome visitors with open arms.

Colonial Architecture in Galle Fort: Stroll through the charming streets of Galle Fort, a UNESCO-listed heritage site, and admire the well-preserved colonial architecture. The fort's historic walls, lighthouses, and charming boutiques offer a delightful experience without any cost.

Kandy Lake and Peradeniya Botanical Gardens: Enjoy a leisurely walk around the picturesque Kandy Lake, located in the heart of the city. Admire the serene surroundings and snap photos of the Temple of the Tooth reflecting on the water. The nearby Peradeniya Botanical Gardens offer a lush escape with a nominal entry fee, showcasing an extensive collection of tropical flora.

Nature Escapes: Embark on hikes and nature walks in places like Ella, Horton Plains National Park, and Sinharaja Forest Reserve. These outdoor adventures present incredible opportunities to explore Sri Lanka's diverse landscapes and encounter its fascinating flora and fauna.

Local Markets: Wander through bustling local markets such as Pettah in Colombo or Kandy Market Square, where you can experience the vibrant atmosphere, sample local street food, and shop for souvenirs and handicrafts at reasonable prices.

Cultural Shows: While some cultural shows may have admission fees, there are often free performances and events held during festivals or special occasions. Keep an eye out for local advertisements to catch a glimpse of traditional dance and music performances.

Picnics and Sunsets: Pack a picnic and head to scenic spots like Diyatha Uyana in Colombo or any of the coastal beaches to enjoy a relaxing afternoon surrounded by nature. Watching the sunset over the Indian Ocean is a priceless experience that won't cost you a cent.

Wildlife Watching: Sri Lanka's national parks and reserves offer incredible wildlife experiences. While safaris may involve fees, you can spot various bird species and animals like monkeys and monitor lizards in places like Udawalawe and Sinharaja without incurring additional costs.

Hiking and Nature Exploration on a Budget

Adam's Peak: Adam's Peak is a popular hiking destination in Sri Lanka. The hike is challenging, but the views from the summit are worth it. You can hike Adam's Peak on a budget by staying in a local guesthouse and packing your own lunch.

Pidurangala Rock: Pidurangala Rock is a lesser-known alternative to Adam's Peak. The hike is shorter and less challenging, but the views are just as stunning. You can hike Pidurangala Rock on a budget by staying in a local guesthouse and packing your own lunch.

Sinhala Rock: Sinhala Rock is a small rock formation that offers stunning views of the surrounding area. The hike is short and easy, making it a great option for budget travelers and families.

Knuckles Mountain Range: The Knuckles Mountain Range is a beautiful mountain range that offers a variety of hiking trails. You can find trails to suit all levels of experience, from easy walks to challenging hikes.

Horton Plains National Park: Horton Plains National Park is a UNESCO World Heritage Site that is home to a variety of wildlife, including elephants, leopards, and birds. There are a number of hiking trails in the park, including the famous World's End viewpoint.

Start your research early: Before you go, do some research on the different hiking trails available. This will help you to choose a trail that is suitable for your fitness level and interests.

Pack light: When you are hiking, it is important to pack light. The hike will become simpler and more pleasurable as a result.

Be prepared for the weather: Sri Lanka has a tropical climate, so be prepared for hot, humid weather. Bring plenty of sunglasses, hats, and sunscreen.

Stay hydrated: It is important to stay hydrated when you are hiking. Water is essential, so make sure to bring plenty and drink often.

Be aware of your surroundings: When you are hiking, be aware of your surroundings. Be on the lookout for wild animals, and be careful of slippery rocks.

Cultural Shows and Festivals

Vesak Festival: Vesak is the most important Buddhist festival in Sri Lanka. It is observed to remember the Buddha's birth, enlightenment, and passing. The festival is held in May or June, and it is a time for people to come together to celebrate their faith. There are many cultural shows and events held during Vesak, including traditional dances, music, and religious ceremonies.

Esala Perahera: The Esala Perahera is a colorful and vibrant Buddhist festival held in Kandy, Sri Lanka. The festival features a procession of elephants, dancers, musicians, and other performers. The Esala Perahera is a UNESCO World Heritage Site, and it is one of the most popular tourist attractions in Sri Lanka.

Kandyan Dances: Kandyan dances are a form of traditional Sri Lankan dance that originated in the Kandy region. The dances are characterized by their intricate footwork, graceful movements, and use of traditional instruments. There are many opportunities to see Kandyan dances in Sri Lanka, including at cultural shows, festivals, and even in some hotels.

Mask Dances: Mask dances are another form of traditional Sri Lankan dance. The dances are performed by dancers wearing elaborate masks and costumes. Mask dances are often performed at festivals and other cultural events.

Sri Lankan Music: Sri Lankan music is a diverse and vibrant blend of traditional and modern influences. There are many different types of Sri Lankan music, including folk music, classical music, and popular music. There are many opportunities to hear Sri Lankan music in Sri Lanka, including at cultural shows, festivals, and even in some restaurants.

Start your research early: Before you go, do some research on the different cultural shows and festivals available. This will help you to choose a show or festival that is suitable for your interests and budget.

Look for free or low-cost events: There are many free or low-cost cultural shows and festivals held in Sri Lanka. Be sure to look for these events when planning your trip.

Book your tickets in advance: If you are planning to attend a popular cultural show or festival, be sure to book your tickets in advance. This will help you to avoid disappointment.

Dress appropriately: When attending a cultural show or festival, it is important to dress appropriately. This means dressing modestly and avoiding revealing clothing.

Be respectful: When attending a cultural show or festival, it is important to be respectful of the local culture. This means being quiet during performances and avoiding taking photos or videos without permission.

CHAPTER 7

Money-Saving Tips and Tricks

Bargaining and Negotiating Prices

Be prepared to bargain: Bargaining is a common practice in Sri Lanka, and it is a great way to save money. Be prepared to haggle over the price of goods and services, and don't be afraid to walk away if you don't get a good deal.

Do your research: Before you start bargaining, do some research on the typical prices for the goods and services you are interested in. This will help you to know what a fair price is and to avoid being overcharged.

Be confident: When you are bargaining, it is important to be confident. If you seem hesitant or unsure, the seller will be less likely to give you a good deal.

Be polite: Even though you are bargaining, it is important to be polite to the seller. This will help to create a good rapport and make the bargaining process more enjoyable.

Be willing to walk away: In the event that you are not pleased with the price, be prepared to walk away. This will show the seller that you are serious about getting a good deal.

Start low: When you are bargaining, start by offering a price that is lower than what you are willing to pay. You will have some negotiating room as a result.

Be patient: Bargaining can be a slow process, so be patient and don't get discouraged.

Use humor: If you are feeling stuck, try using humor to break the ice. This can help to create a more relaxed atmosphere and make the bargaining process more enjoyable.

Trust your gut: If you feel like you are being taken advantage of, trust your gut and walk away. There are plenty of other sellers out there who will be willing to give you a fair deal.

Using Public Facilities Wisely

Use public transportation: Public transportation is a great way to get around Sri Lanka and to save money. There are buses, trains, and tuk-tuks (three-wheeled taxis) available in most cities and towns.

Visit free attractions: There are many free attractions in Sri Lanka, such as temples, beaches, and national parks. These are a great way to see the country and save money on your trip.

Cook your own meals: If you are on a tight budget, you can save money by cooking your own meals. There are many affordable grocery stores in Sri Lanka, and you can find fresh produce and spices at local markets.

Consider staying in a hostel: Hostels are an excellent way to save money on lodging. They offer shared rooms and bathrooms, and they are a great way to meet other travelers.

Use free Wi-Fi: There are many places in Sri Lanka where you can find free Wi-Fi. This is a great way to stay connected and to save money on your data plan.

Be respectful of the local culture: When using public facilities in Sri Lanka, it is important to be respectful of the local culture. This means dressing modestly and avoiding taking photos or videos without permission.

Be aware of your surroundings: When you are using public facilities, be aware of your surroundings. Be on the lookout for pickpockets and other criminals.

Keep your belongings safe: When you are using public facilities, keep your belongings safe. This means carrying your valuables in a secure bag or pocket.

Be patient: Public facilities in Sri Lanka can be crowded and chaotic. Be patient and don't get frustrated.

Have fun!: Sri Lanka is a beautiful country with a lot to offer. Use public facilities wisely and have a great time!

Understanding Local Customs to Avoid Extra Expenses

Be aware of the local dress code: Sri Lanka is a conservative country, so it is important to be aware of the local dress code. This means dressing modestly and avoiding revealing clothing.

Be respectful of the local culture: When interacting with locals, it is important to be respectful of the local culture. This means avoiding making rude gestures or comments, and it also means being mindful of your personal space.

Learn some basic Sinhala or Tamil phrases: Learning some basic Sinhala or Tamil phrases can help you to communicate with locals and avoid misunderstandings.

Be aware of the tipping culture: Tipping is not expected in Sri Lanka, but it is appreciated in some cases. If you do choose to tip, a small amount is sufficient.

Be aware of the religious customs: Sri Lanka is a multi-religious country, so it is important to be aware of the religious customs of the different groups. This means avoiding wearing revealing clothing in religious places, and it also means being respectful of religious practices.

Do your research: Before you go, do some research on the local customs of Sri Lanka. You can avoid offending any cultures by doing this.

Ask questions: Never be hesitant to ask questions if you are uncertain about something. Locals are usually happy to help you understand their culture.

Be open-minded: Sri Lanka is a beautiful country with a rich culture. Be open-minded to new experiences and be respectful of the local culture.

CHAPTER 8

Safety and Travel Precautions

General Safety Tips for Tourists

Be aware of your surroundings: This is probably the most important safety tip for any tourist, but it is especially important in Sri Lanka. Be aware of your surroundings at all times, and be on the lookout for pickpockets and other criminals.

Don't carry valuables: If you can, avoid carrying valuables with you when you are out and about. If you do need to carry valuables, keep them in a secure bag or pocket that is close to your body.

Be careful at night: Nighttime is generally considered to be more dangerous than daytime in Sri Lanka. If you are out at night, be sure to stay in well-lit areas and avoid walking alone.

Always go with your instinct; if something doesn't feel right, it probably is. Don't be afraid to walk away from a situation or to ask for help.

Drink bottled water: Tap water in Sri Lanka is not safe to drink, so be sure to drink bottled water instead.

Be careful with food: Street food in Sri Lanka can be delicious, but it is important to be careful. Some street food vendors may not use safe practices, so it is best to avoid food that has been sitting out in the open or that is not cooked thoroughly.

Use common sense: This is probably the most important safety tip of all. Use common sense when you are in Sri Lanka and avoid putting yourself in dangerous situations.

Stay in a safe area: If you are staying in a hotel, be sure to choose a hotel in a safe area.

Don't flash your valuables: Don't wear flashy jewelry or carry expensive cameras or phones in public.

Be aware of scams: There are a number of scams that target tourists in Sri Lanka. Be aware of these scams and be sure to research them before you go.

Report any suspicious activity: If you see anything suspicious, be sure to report it to the police.

Health and Hygiene Precautions

Get vaccinated: Before you go to Sri Lanka, be sure to get vaccinated against the following diseases:

Hepatitis A

Hepatitis B

Typhoid

Polio

Diphtheria

Tetanus

Malaria (if you are visiting rural areas)

Wash your hands often: This is the single most important thing you can do to stay healthy while traveling. Wash your hands with soap and water for at least 20 seconds, especially after using the bathroom, before eating, and after being in contact with someone who is sick.

Drink bottled water: Tap water in Sri Lanka is not safe to drink, so be sure to drink bottled water instead.

Be careful with food: Street food in Sri Lanka can be delicious, but it is important to be careful. Some street food vendors may not use safe practices, so it is best to avoid food that has been sitting out in the open or that is not cooked thoroughly.

Use sunscreen: The sun in Sri Lanka can be very strong, so be sure to use sunscreen with an SPF of 30 or higher.

Cover up: If you are going to be spending time in the sun, be sure to cover up with long sleeves and pants.

Take malaria medication: If you are visiting rural areas, you should take malaria medication. Make sure to discuss which medication is best for you with your doctor.

See a doctor before you go: If you have any health concerns, be sure to see a doctor before you go to Sri Lanka. They can give you advice on what vaccinations you need and what other precautions you should take.

Go to a doctor if you get sick: If you get sick while you are in Sri Lanka, be sure to go to a doctor. There are many good hospitals in Sri Lanka, and you will be able to get the care you need.

Drink plenty of water: It's crucial to drink plenty of water, especially if you're spending time in the sun. Avoid sugary beverages and drink lots of water.

Listen to your body: If you are feeling tired or rundown, take a break. Don't push yourself too hard.

Have fun!: Sri Lanka is a beautiful country with a lot to offer. Enjoy your trip and be safe!

Avoiding Scams and Tourist Traps

Be aware of the most common scams: There are a number of scams that target tourists in Sri Lanka. Be aware of these scams and be sure to research them before you go. Some of the most common scams include:

The gem scam: This scam involves a local offering to take you to a gem mine or shop where you can buy gems at a discounted price. However, the gems are usually fake or overpriced.

The tuk-tuk scam: This scam involves a tuk-tuk driver taking you on a long and expensive ride. The driver may also take you to places that you don't want to go or that are not safe.

The fake taxi scam: This scam involves a taxi driver taking you to a fake taxi stand where you will be overcharged for your ride.

The restaurant scam: This scam involves a restaurant charging you exorbitant prices for food and drinks. The restaurant may also try to add hidden charges to your bill.

Always go with your instinct; if something doesn't feel right, it probably is. Don't be afraid to walk away from a situation or to ask for help.

Do your research: Before you go, do some research on the most common scams in Sri Lanka. This will help you to avoid falling victim to one of these scams.

Be careful with your belongings: Keep your belongings close to you at all times, especially in crowded areas.

Don't flash your money: Don't carry large amounts of cash with you and don't flash your money around.

Be mindful of your surroundings: At all times, especially in crowded situations, be mindful of your surroundings.

Report any suspicious activity: If you see anything suspicious, be sure to report it to the police.

CHAPTER 9

Sustainable Tourism in Sri Lanka

Responsible Travel Practices

As a responsible traveler, it's essential to prioritize sustainable and ethical practices to preserve the natural and cultural beauty of Sri Lanka. By adopting these responsible travel practices, you can ensure that your journey positively impacts the local communities, the environment, and the future of the destination:

Respect Local Customs and Traditions: Embrace the cultural diversity of Sri Lanka by respecting local customs, traditions, and beliefs. Dress modestly when visiting temples and sacred sites, and always remove your shoes before entering religious places. Learning a few phrases in Sinhala or Tamil to greet locals will also be appreciated and show your respect for their language.

Support Local Communities: Opt for local businesses, homestays, and locally owned guesthouses, as they directly contribute to the livelihoods of the communities. Engaging with local guides and artisans for tours and shopping not only enhances your experience but also supports sustainable tourism.

Reduce Plastic Waste: Sri Lanka faces challenges with plastic pollution. As a responsible traveler, carry a reusable water bottle and refill it whenever possible. Say no to single-use plastic bags and dispose of waste properly. Participate in beach clean-ups and other initiatives that promote environmental conservation.

Preserve Wildlife and Natural Habitats: When visiting national parks and reserves, follow the rules and guidelines provided by park authorities to protect the wildlife and their habitats. Avoid getting too close to animals, refrain from feeding them, and never disturb their natural behavior.

Choose Eco-Friendly Activities: Opt for eco-friendly activities that promote conservation and minimize environmental impact. Participate in nature walks, birdwatching tours, or tree-planting initiatives that contribute to preserving Sri Lanka's unique biodiversity.

Conserve Water and Energy: Practice water and energy conservation during your stay by taking short showers, turning off lights and air conditioning when not in use, and reusing towels to reduce laundry demand.

Minimize Single-Use Plastics: Bring a reusable shopping bag and avoid accepting plastic bags from stores. Carry a reusable straw and utensils to reduce single-use plastic waste while dining.

Responsible Wildlife Encounters: If you wish to observe wildlife, choose responsible operators that prioritize the welfare of animals. Avoid attractions that involve animal exploitation or captive wildlife.

Respect Nature: Leave no trace when exploring natural areas. Avoid littering and stay on marked trails to minimize your impact on the environment.

Support Conservation Projects: Consider supporting local conservation organizations or projects that work towards protecting Sri Lanka's wildlife and natural heritage. Your contributions can make a positive difference in preserving the island's treasures for future generations.

Supporting Local Communities and Conservation Efforts

Supporting local communities and conservation efforts is a vital aspect of responsible travel, especially in a country like Sri Lanka, where the preservation of cultural heritage and natural biodiversity is crucial. Here are some meaningful ways you can contribute to the well-being of local communities and the environment during your visit:

Choose Local Businesses: Opt for locally owned accommodations, restaurants, and tour operators. By supporting local businesses, you directly contribute to the livelihoods of community members and help foster a sustainable economy.

Buy Local Products: Purchase locally made handicrafts, souvenirs, and products during your trip. Buying from local artisans and markets empowers the local community and preserves traditional craftsmanship.

Engage with Local Guides: Hire local guides and experts to enhance your travel experience. Their knowledge and insights provide a deeper understanding of the destination's culture, history, and natural wonders.

Participate in Community-Based Tourism: Seek out community-based tourism initiatives that directly involve local communities. These programs often include homestays, cultural experiences, and guided tours led by community members, allowing you to connect with locals on a personal level.

Volunteer for Conservation Projects: Consider dedicating some of your time to volunteer for conservation efforts in Sri Lanka. Numerous organizations work towards protecting the island's wildlife, marine life, and natural habitats. Contributing to such projects can make a meaningful impact on the environment.

Join Responsible Wildlife Tours: If you're interested in wildlife encounters, choose tours and activities that prioritize the welfare of animals and respect their natural behavior. Avoid attractions that involve captive wildlife or contribute to animal exploitation.

Support Marine Conservation: Sri Lanka's marine ecosystems are valuable and fragile. Contribute to marine conservation by participating in beach clean-ups, coral reef monitoring, or supporting organizations that work to protect the ocean.

Respect Local Customs and Environment: Be mindful of local customs, traditions, and beliefs. Respect sacred sites, wildlife, and natural habitats. Refrain from littering and minimize your environmental impact during your travels.

Make Responsible Choices: Make responsible choices during your trip, such as conserving water and energy, minimizing waste, and reducing plastic usage. Small actions can collectively contribute to sustainable tourism.

Educate and Raise Awareness: Share your experiences with others and raise awareness about responsible travel practices. Encourage fellow travelers to make conscious choices that benefit local communities and conservation efforts.

CHAPTER 10

Basic Local Phrases and Cultural Etiquette

Useful Phrases in Sinhala and Tamil

When visiting Sri Lanka, learning a few useful phrases in both Sinhala and Tamil can greatly enhance your travel experience and show respect for the local culture. Here are some common phrases in both languages:

Sinhala Phrases:

Hello - ▢▢▢▢▢▢▢ (Aayubowan)

Good morning - ▢▢▢ ▢▢▢▢▢▢▢ (Suba Udaesak)

Thank you - ▢▢▢▢▢▢▢ (Sthuthi)

Yes - ▢▢▢ (Owa)

No - ▢▢▢ (Nae-tha)

Please - ▢▢▢▢▢ (Karannaa)

Excuse me - ▢▢▢▢ ▢▢▢▢▢ (Samaana karannaa)

How much? - ▢▢▢▢ ▢▢▢▢▢▢▢▢ (Muluvina balanak)

Where is…? - …▢▢▢▢ ▢▢▢▢▢▢▢ (Kohe we-laa-vak)

I don't understand - මට තේරෙන්නේ නැහැ (Mama danavath nae-tha)

Tamil Phrases:

Hello - வணக்கம் (Vanakkam)

Good morning - காலை வணக்கம் (Kaalai vanakkam)

Thank you - நன்றி (Nandri)

Yes - ஆம் (Aam)

No - இல்லை (Illai)

Please - தயவு செய்து (Thayavu seithu)

Excuse me - மன்னிக்கவும் (Mannikkavum)

How much? - எவ்வளவு பணம்? (Evvallavu panam?)

Where is...? - ...எங்கு உள்ளது? (...Engu ullathu?)

I don't understand - எனக்கு புரியவில்லை (Enakku puriyavillai)

Learning and using these phrases will be appreciated by the locals and will make your interactions more enjoyable and meaningful during your travels in Sri Lanka.

Cultural Dos and Don'ts for Respectful Travel

To ensure a respectful and culturally sensitive travel experience in Sri Lanka, it's essential to be mindful of certain dos and don'ts. Embracing local customs and traditions while avoiding any inadvertent offense will help you build positive connections with the Sri Lankan people and create lasting memories. Here are some cultural dos and don'ts for respectful travel:

Dos:

Greeting: Greet locals with a warm "Ayubowan" (in Sinhala) or "Vanakkam" (in Tamil) to show respect and politeness.

Modest Dressing: When visiting temples and other religious sites, dress modestly by covering your shoulders and knees. Remove hats and shoes before entering temples as a sign of respect.

Asking Permission: Always ask for permission before taking photographs of people, especially monks and locals in rural areas.

Accepting Hospitality: If invited to a local's home, accept the hospitality graciously. It is customary to remove your shoes before entering a Sri Lankan home.

Using Your Right Hand: Use your right hand for eating and giving and receiving items, as the left hand is considered unclean.

Respecting Religious Sites: Show reverence at religious sites, refrain from loud conversation, and turn off mobile phones. Do not touch or climb on statues, stupas, or other sacred objects.

Conserving Water: Sri Lanka can experience water scarcity, so use water sparingly, especially in rural areas.

Tipping: Tipping is not mandatory but appreciated in Sri Lanka. It is customary to tip waitstaff, drivers, and tour guides if you are satisfied with their service.

Haggling: Bargaining is common in markets, but do so with a friendly attitude and without being overly aggressive.

Learning Basic Phrases: Learn a few basic phrases in Sinhala or Tamil to communicate with locals. Your efforts will be appreciated.

Don'ts:

Public Display of Affection: Avoid public displays of affection, as they are not common in Sri Lankan culture.

Disrespecting Religious Symbols: Avoid wearing clothing with images of Buddha or other religious symbols, as it is considered disrespectful.

Feet Pointing: Avoid pointing your feet at people, especially religious figures or elders, as it is seen as impolite.

Disrespecting Monks: Show reverence to Buddhist monks by offering them the right of way and refraining from physical contact.

Touching People's Heads: Avoid touching people's heads, as it is considered disrespectful in Sri Lankan culture.

Public Nudity: Public nudity is not acceptable in Sri Lanka and may lead to legal consequences.

Insulting the National Flag or Anthem: The national flag and anthem are revered symbols, and any disrespect may lead to legal consequences.

Over-tipping: While tipping is appreciated, excessive tipping may not be culturally appropriate.

Distributing Gifts to Children: Avoid giving money or gifts to children, as it can encourage a begging culture.

Littering: Respect the environment by not littering. Dispose of waste properly and participate in beach clean-ups if possible.

By adhering to these cultural dos and don'ts, you can ensure a respectful and enriching travel experience in Sri Lanka, forming genuine connections with the local culture and leaving a positive impact on the communities you visit.

CHAPTER 11

Packing Essentials for a Budget Trip

Clothing and Weather Considerations

Sri Lanka's climate varies throughout the year, and packing appropriate clothing is essential to stay comfortable during your trip. Here are clothing and weather considerations for all seasons in Sri Lanka:

1. Dry Season (December to March):

Weather: The dry season brings sunny and warm weather to most parts of the country. Coastal areas and lowlands experience pleasant temperatures, while the hill country remains cool.

Clothing:

Lightweight, breathable fabrics such as cotton and linen are ideal for coastal regions and lowlands.

Light sweaters or jackets may be needed for the hill country during the evenings, as temperatures can get cooler.

In order to protect oneself from the harsh sun, don't forget to take sunscreen, sunglasses, and a hat.

2. Inter-Monsoon Season (April and September to November):

Weather: The inter-monsoon seasons bring a mix of sunny days and occasional rain showers. The weather is generally warm and humid.

Clothing:

Pack lightweight clothing suitable for warm weather and occasional rain. Quick-drying fabrics are useful in case of sudden showers.

A compact umbrella or a light rain jacket can come in handy.

3. Southwest Monsoon (May to August):

Weather: During the southwest monsoon, the southwestern coast and the hill country experience heavier rainfall.

Clothing:

Bring waterproof clothing, such as a raincoat or poncho, to stay dry during downpours.

Closed-toe shoes or waterproof sandals are recommended to navigate wet and muddy terrain.

4. Northeast Monsoon (October to January):

Weather: The northeastern regions, including the Cultural Triangle and the east coast, experience rainfall during the northeast monsoon.

Clothing:

Similar to the southwest monsoon, prepare for rainy days with waterproof gear.

Light layers can be useful as temperatures remain warm even during the rain.

General Clothing Tips:

In conservative areas or when visiting temples, avoid revealing clothing and opt for modest attire covering your shoulders and knees.

Comfortable walking shoes or sandals are essential for exploring Sri Lanka's diverse landscapes.

If you plan to hike in the hill country, bring sturdy footwear and warm clothing, as temperatures can drop, especially at higher altitudes.

Consider packing a swimsuit, as Sri Lanka's beautiful beaches and resorts invite you to take a refreshing dip in the ocean or pool.

Regardless of the season, packing a small travel umbrella, a reusable water bottle, and insect repellent are wise decisions for any trip to Sri Lanka. By being prepared for various weather conditions, you can fully enjoy your adventures in this captivating island paradise.

Essential Items and Gadgets

When traveling to Sri Lanka, packing the right essentials and gadgets can enhance your comfort, safety, and overall travel experience. Here's a list of must-have items and gadgets to consider for your trip:

Essential Items:

Valid Passport and Travel Documents: Ensure your passport has at least six months of validity from your planned departure date. Don't forget to carry your travel insurance details and any necessary visas.

Printed Copies of Important Documents: Have printed copies of your passport, travel insurance, accommodation reservations, and emergency contact information.

Cash and Credit/Debit Cards: Carry some Sri Lankan rupees in cash for emergencies and places that might not accept cards. Notify your bank about your travel dates to avoid any card issues.

Daypack or Backpack: A lightweight daypack is essential for carrying water, snacks, and essentials during day trips and hikes.

Reusable Water Bottle: Bring a reusable water bottle with you to stay hydrated and cut down on plastic trash. Many hotels and restaurants offer filtered water refills.

Travel Adapter: Sri Lanka uses the Type D, M, and G electrical sockets. Make sure to bring the appropriate travel adapter for your devices.

Universal Plug Adapter with USB Ports: A universal adapter with USB ports allows you to charge multiple devices simultaneously.

Power Bank: Keep your gadgets charged on the go with a reliable power bank, especially during long journeys or outdoor activities.

First Aid Kit: Pack a basic first aid kit with band-aids, antiseptic cream, painkillers, and any necessary medications.

Sunscreen and Mosquito Repellent: Protect your skin from the sun's rays and insect bites while exploring.

Sunglasses and Hat: Shield your eyes and face from the sun with a pair of sunglasses and a wide-brimmed hat.

Towel or Sarong: A lightweight and quick-drying towel or sarong can be handy for beach days or impromptu swims.

Gadgets:

Smartphone: Your smartphone is a versatile tool for navigation, communication, and capturing memories.

Camera: Bring a quality camera to capture the breathtaking landscapes and vibrant culture of Sri Lanka.

Portable Wi-Fi Router or SIM Card: Stay connected and access the internet with a portable Wi-Fi router or a local SIM card.

Travel Apps: Download useful travel apps such as maps, translation, currency converter, and weather forecasts.

E-Reader: If you enjoy reading, an e-reader saves space and weight compared to physical books.

Portable Bluetooth Speaker: Enjoy music or podcasts on the go with a compact Bluetooth speaker.

Waterproof Phone Case or Pouch: Protect your phone from water, sand, and dust during outdoor activities.

Portable Flashlight or Headlamp: A small flashlight or headlamp can be useful for navigating dark areas or during power outages.

Travel Locks: Keep your belongings secure with TSA-approved travel locks for luggage and daypacks.

Noise-Canceling Earphones or Headphones: Block out background noise and enjoy your music or podcasts during flights or long journeys.

Remember to pack these items based on your specific needs and preferences, as well as the activities you plan to undertake in Sri Lanka. Having the right essentials and gadgets will ensure a smooth and enjoyable adventure on this beautiful island.

Packing Light and Smart

Packing light and smart is a valuable approach when traveling to Sri Lanka. It not only reduces the burden of carrying heavy luggage but also provides more flexibility and ease during your journey. Here are some tips to help you pack light and smart for your Sri Lankan adventure:

1. Research the Weather: Check the weather forecast for your travel dates and the regions you plan to visit. Pack clothes that suit the season and climate, focusing on lightweight and versatile pieces.

2. Mix and Match Clothing: Pack clothing items that can be mixed and matched to create multiple outfits. Stick to neutral colors that can be easily paired and layered.

3. Choose Lightweight Fabrics: Opt for lightweight and breathable fabrics, such as cotton and linen, which are comfortable in Sri Lanka's warm and humid climate.

4. Pack Travel-Sized Toiletries: Use travel-sized toiletries to save space and weight. Consider leaving behind items that can be easily purchased at local stores.

5. Use Packing Cubes or Compression Bags: Organize your belongings with packing cubes or compression bags to maximize space and keep things neat and tidy.

6. Minimize Shoes: Limit the number of shoes you pack. A comfortable pair for walking or hiking and a pair of sandals or flip-flops for casual wear should be sufficient.

7. Wear Your Bulkiest Items: If you need to bring bulkier items, such as a jacket or sneakers, wear them during your travel to save space in your luggage.

8. Pack Multi-Functional Items: Choose items that serve multiple purposes, such as a scarf that can double as a shawl or a sarong that can be used as a towel or beach cover-up.

9. Limit Electronics: Bring only essential electronics, such as your smartphone, camera, and necessary chargers. Consider leaving non-essential gadgets at home.

10. Roll Your Clothes: Rolling clothes instead of folding them can help save space and reduce wrinkles.

11. Laundry Options: Many accommodations in Sri Lanka offer laundry facilities or laundry services. Consider doing laundry during your trip to reduce the amount of clothing you need to pack.

12. Pack Reusable Items: Bring reusable items like a water bottle, utensils, and a tote bag to reduce waste and minimize your environmental impact.

13. Check Baggage Allowance: Be aware of your airline's baggage allowance to avoid excess baggage fees. If possible, stick to carry-on luggage to save time at the airport.

By packing light and smart, you'll enjoy a more hassle-free and enjoyable experience in Sri Lanka, allowing you to focus on exploring the country's beauty and immersing yourself in its vibrant culture.

CONCLUSION AND FINAL TIPS

Recap of Key Points

Introduction to Sri Lanka: Sri Lanka is a captivating island paradise in the Indian Ocean, known for its stunning landscapes, rich culture, and warm hospitality.

Geography and Climate: Sri Lanka's diverse geography offers everything from golden beaches to lush mountains. The weather varies with different regions and seasons.

Cultural Diversity and Traditions: Sri Lanka's culture is a blend of Sinhalese, Tamil, and colonial influences, resulting in colorful festivals, ancient traditions, and warm customs.

Top Attractions and Must-Visit Places: Explore ancient cities like Anuradhapura and Polonnaruwa, visit stunning beaches in Mirissa and Unawatuna, and experience the lush beauty of Ella and the hill country.

Choosing the Right Time to Visit: Consider the weather and your preferences for outdoor activities when planning your trip. Sri Lanka can be visited year-round, but different regions have distinct best times to visit.

Getting to Sri Lanka: Bandaranaike International Airport in Colombo is the main international gateway. Sri Lanka is well-connected by air, and domestic transportation options make it easy to explore the country.

Budget-Friendly Accommodations: Hostels, guesthouses, and home-stays offer affordable and authentic stays. Look for options run by locals to support the community.

Free and Low-Cost Attractions: Enjoy the beauty of Sri Lanka without spending much by visiting stunning beaches, exploring ancient ruins, and engaging in free cultural experiences.

Responsible Travel Practices: Respect local customs, support local communities and conservation efforts, reduce plastic waste, and conserve water and energy.

Cultural Dos and Don'ts for Respectful Travel: Show respect for local customs, traditions, and religious sites. Dress modestly when necessary, and be mindful of your actions and interactions.

Essential Items and Gadgets: Pack essential travel items, such as a valid passport, cash, reusable water bottle, power bank, first aid kit, universal adapter, and appropriate clothing for the weather.

Packing Light and Smart: Research the weather, pack lightweight fabrics, mix and match clothing, and use packing cubes. Minimize electronics and bring only essential items.

By keeping these key points in mind, you'll be well-prepared for an incredible and budget-friendly journey to Sri Lanka.

Enjoy your travels and immerse yourself in the beauty and culture of this enchanting island!

Embracing the Adventure: Final Thoughts on Budget Travel in Sri Lanka

Embracing the adventure of budget travel in Sri Lanka is a journey filled with enchanting landscapes, cultural richness, and authentic experiences. As you venture through this captivating island, you'll discover that the beauty of Sri Lanka extends far beyond its breathtaking vistas. It lies in the warmth of its people, the vibrant tapestry of traditions, and the cherished memories you create along the way.

As a budget traveler, you have the unique opportunity to connect with the heart and soul of Sri Lanka. Engaging with local communities, supporting sustainable initiatives, and immersing yourself in the island's diverse culture will enrich your journey and leave a positive impact.

From exploring ancient ruins and basking on sun-kissed beaches to hiking through lush tea plantations and tasting mouthwatering cuisine, Sri Lanka offers a treasure trove of experiences without breaking the bank. You'll find that sometimes the simplest pleasures, like watching a mesmerizing sunset or savoring a cup of Ceylon tea, are the most rewarding.

Throughout your adventure, remember to be open-minded, respectful, and appreciative of the local way of life. Embrace the joy of spontaneous encounters, the excitement of trying something new, and the humbling moments that connect you with the heart of Sri Lanka.

As you journey through this enchanting land on a budget, cherish the memories you create, the friendships you forge, and the experiences that shape your understanding of this beautiful world we share. Your budget travel in Sri Lanka will be a transformative experience, one that leaves you with a deep appreciation for the wonders of the island and a yearning to return for more.

So, pack your sense of wonder, curiosity, and a spirit of adventure as you embark on this budget-friendly escapade in Sri Lanka. May your journey be filled with joy, discovery, and the kind of enchantment that only Sri Lanka can offer. Safe travels and happy exploring!

Printed in Great Britain
by Amazon